How You Can

*MOVE
BEYOND*

PROCRASTINATION

by

Virginia M. Granger

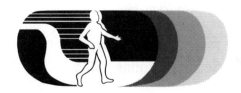

MOVING ON PUBLICATIONS
Tempe, Arizona

How You Can Move Beyond Procrastination
by Virginia M. Granger

Published by Moving On Publications
Address inquiries to:
924 East Westchester Drive
Tempe, Arizona 85283-3037

Printed and bound in the United States
of America

First printing 1991.
Second printing 1992.

Includes index
Printed in easy-to-read type
ISBN 0-9627840-0-1

Library of Congress Catalog Card
Number: 90-92233

To my son, Joe,
and my daughter, Carol...
for their belief in me.
There was never a word of criticism
from them when I took detours
and lost my way.

I wish to express my thanks, love, and deep appreciation to the people who have supported me in this project:

Velma Buddemeyer, Mary Lee Madison, Joe Martindell, Robin Morris, Marjorie Riegel, Billie Reynolds, and Evert Vollmar.

I am also grateful for the work of my editor, Carol Vollmar, of The Word Works, Los Osos, California. Her consistent discernment and skill in the organization, design, and application of this manuscript enhanced the final form.

CONTENTS

CONTENTS

PREFACE

If you suffer from procrastination, meet a fellow sufferer. When I was a child, I dreamed of becoming a writer. Sixty-seven years after the birth of this dream, I have written my first book. The irony is that the topic of this book explains why it took me so long to get here.

How You Can Move Beyond Procrastination began as a ten-page chapter in a separate, yet-to-be published book. This chapter, originally titled **"Procrastination,"** nagged and tugged at me and seemed to want more attention than the rest. It grew from ten pages to twenty, then thirty... It was as if this chapter begged to be the *star*. Finally, it jumped out of the original book and grew into the form you hold in your hands today.

I loved writing this book, and I will miss it. It was difficult for me to close it off and write "The End." But, as I worked to perfect the manuscript, I realized I had given into procrastination again. Perfectionism is a form of procrastination, and perfectionism had become my greatest nemesis. Had I not recognized this, my book may never have been published.

I am amazed at the many ways there are to procrastinate, and I am excited to share the solutions with you.

Is there anyone who does not procrastinate? More importantly, does procrastination cause *you* misery and unhappiness?

If you are not reaching your full potential, this book is for you.

SECTION I

IT WAS PROCRASTINATION ALL THE TIME!

CHAPTER 1

BREAK OUT
OF YOUR SHELL!

Once I owned an aviary of cockatiels. They are
my favorite of all the pet birds. Cockatiels are
small parrot-like birds that have bright-orange
circular patches on their cheeks. These little birds
are colorful, friendly, and talented. Each has its
own fascinating and charismatic personality. They
chirp their little hearts out, singing their own
natural songs. They can be taught to talk and

whistle your favorite tune as well. I found the cockatiel easy to breed. But, sometimes one or more of the eggs from my birds' clutches didn't hatch. With disappointment, I opened these eggs. Some were infertile but others held perfectly formed birds—dead in their shells.

I grieved over each little bird. The other chicks had pecked their way out; why hadn't these? My sadness puzzled me. As time passed, I realized that my grief was not only for the dead birds, but for myself as well. I, too, felt as if I were in a shell and couldn't break free. These birds never sang their songs...neither had I. How sad it would be if I should die never having fully lived.

Have you wondered why some people move with apparent ease, chalking up one success after another while others never do? You can analyze, hypothesize and rationalize, but the reason is most people procrastinate.

How about you? Would you like to know if procrastination is affecting your life? The following test is a good tool to identify the types of procrastination that give you problems. You also can use it to check your progress as you apply the solutions offered in this book.

PROCRASTINATION SELF-TEST

1. Are you putting off tackling a project or important goal until there is no stress in your life?

2. Do you need to get everything in order before you go to work in earnest?

3. Have you put your life on hold while you wait for someone else to do something?

4. Are you a couch potato?

5. Are you a bookworm?

6. Do you blame others because your life is unhappy?

7. Do you feel life is fleeting from you?

8. Do you have difficulty stopping work?

9. Are you one of those people who takes on so much responsibility that you invariably have to ask for someone's help?

10. Are you maintaining a dependent relationship with the hope that another will take care of you?

11. Conversely, are you pouring your life into the life of another as a caretaker?

12. How prompt are you at getting out of bed in the morning?

13. Are you often depressed?

14. Do you complain about being tired?

Perhaps you think some of these questions have nothing to do with procrastination. If so, procrastination may be fooling you. As you read this book, the reasons for these questions will become clear.

Consider question 2. Do you rearrange, clean, organize, tinker, make phone calls, write letters, run errands, and do you say, "I'll get these little bothersome things out of the way first, then I'll settle down to some serious work?" If so, you are procrastinating!

Can you see the clever psychology behind question 9? The person who takes pity on the over-worked procrastinator inevitably finishes the job.

How did you answer question 12? Do you use a "snooze" alarm? If so, you may like the idea that you can turn it off and crawl back under the covers until it arouses you again. I believe the only purpose of the snooze alarm is to teach you to procrastinate.

If you answered yes to question 13, I encourage you to read "Set Your Goals," in Chapter 7. An abandoned goal can throw you into a deeply depressed state. You may not be aware that you are grieving over dead hopes.

Question 14 is tricky. Did you know that you can be more exhausted if you do not reach your goal than if you do? It takes more energy to procrastinate than it does to complete a project.

Some people are not too concerned that they procrastinate. However, if procrastination causes unhappiness and misery for you, take heart. There is a cure! You will learn how to recognize procrastination and to change your behavior and whip it once and for all!

Procrastination appears to be enticing and seductive while, in truth, it is treacherous. Like a disease, it has a gradual, cumulative effect and establishes itself in your nature before you are aware.

Procrastination can be broken into three categories. There are no distinct lines between these categories, so you may find that you fit into more than one.

1. Some people never finish anything because they never start.

If people have no hope for success, they say, "Why bother?" They blame their problems on something or someone else. Things always happen *to* them—they don't get the breaks; they are unlucky; they had an unhappy childhood; it's the moon, the stars, or fate, but never themselves. These people become bored and boredom is an intolerable state. Consequently, they subconsciously create chaos and havoc just to feel alive. If you observe these people closely, you will see they are expert crisis creators.

Still others never get started because they fear change. They play it safe and hold on to their old ways.

You cannot expect your life to change until you change your habits. When you change your habits, you will experience a new lifestyle. You will not spend your hours in the same way; you will associate with new people; you won't do the same work; and your image of yourself will improve. This will be a drastic rearrangement in both your inner and outer life. Consequently, you may become fearful and think your life is falling apart.

Ask yourself if you want all these changes, because they are inevitable. If you keep faith in yourself and apply the success methods in this book, you will see that your life isn't falling apart; it's coming together.

2. Some people start and quit before they finish.

Every human being has dreams that yearn to become reality. It is a long way from dreams to reality, and some never move beyond the dream stage.

An excellent example is the "do-it-yourselfer" who dreams of remodelling his home and starts with enthusiasm and dedication but quits before he realizes his dream. His wife nags, begs and quarrels at him to finish the job, but to no avail. An enterprising handyman cashed in on the habits of these procrastinators with this ad: "Handyman. I can do anything your husband can, only I'll do it now."

My Uncle Lee was a classic case. When he was twenty, he began to build a new house for his bride-to-be, but she broke the engagement and he never married.

The last time I saw Uncle Lee, I was eight years old and he was in his fifties. Our family spent half a day travelling to his farm in our Model T Ford. He welcomed us warmly, saying, "I'm proud to see you. I fixed up the house for your visit." I looked around and wondered what he was talking about. Unpacked boxes were stacked against the walls. They looked like they had been there since he moved in. He had framed the door and window openings, but he had never gotten around to hanging the doors between the rooms or putting in the window glass and screens.

When Uncle Lee died, the house was still unfinished.

At a recent yard sale, I found a piece of cut fabric with the pattern still pinned to it. I asked the owner about it, and she said "I never got around to finishing it. Someone else can do it."

Whether we abandon a minor project or abandon our life-long dreams, the damage is the same. We have adopted a way of living that causes great pain. We are like the stillborn bird in its shell; our dreams are never realized.

3. Others start and work and work and never finish.

There are those who are afraid to let go of a project while there is one bit more they can do to improve it. *The perfectionist syndrome has taken over.* Because they want a masterpiece, they become addicted to their work and never realize the finished result. This was the trap I fell into while writing this book.

If you feel the need to be perfect, you will experience anxiety and stress that will block your creativity and reduce your productivity. Procrastination will become your friend: a constant companion that reminds you of all you have to do. You could be left owning a package of undone things that you would miss if you finished. Procrastination means never saying "goodbye" to anything.

WHY DO WE DO IT?

Why do some of us employ these tactics in our daily lives? The major reason is that we hope things will change without any action on our part. We assume that things will take care of themselves in time or that others will take care of them for us. For example, some people wait an inordinate amount of time for a physical ailment to clear up on its own. Sometimes they wait so long they lose their health, their teeth, their eyesight or their lives.

Some managers avoid dealing with a difficult employee, adopting the rationale that he or she may improve. Meanwhile, the employee is undermining morale and disrupting production.

Instead of fixing or leaving their miserable marriages, thousands of people choose to stay to the end of their lives, thinking their relationships will improve in time. The longer they wait for things to change, the less drive they have to make any changes, so they wait it out. Ken Dychtwald, in his book, *Age Wave*, tells about a woman who wanted to divorce her husband of fifty-two years. She admitted she hadn't loved him for the last twenty-two years. When she learned that the life expectancy of Americans had increased significantly, she realized she could have another twenty good years left. So she divorced her husband shortly after her seventy-ninth birthday. She finally stopped waiting and went into action before her life was over.

Many people struggle with their debts and live in poverty because they continue day after day to apply the same methods to their work and their lives. They fantasize a life of wealth when they hit a jackpot, win the lottery or inherit a fortune *someday.*

CHAPTER 2

DO YOU THINK
YOU HAVE FOREVER?

There are two ways to get to the top of an oak tree. One is to climb it, the other is to sit on an acorn and wait. All too many of us choose to sit and wait. Since we believe there is plenty of time, we are not too concerned about doing things now.

I certainly thought I had plenty of time when I was young. I was born the early part of the century in Atlanta, Georgia and lived my first ten years in the south. When I was a child, I admired the thin, beautiful flappers. "That's how I want to look when I grow up," I told myself. I also wanted to become Miss America. But, I didn't come close. I was fat from childhood until I was over sixty years old. How could anyone be thin when they ate such "wonderful" southern food? Mama served fried chicken, ham, biscuits and gravy, corn bread, candied yams, and pecan pie! No room for anything as foolish as salad.

Years passed. Styles changed. I gave up on the Miss America contest, but, I still longed to be thin. I always intended to start my diet on Monday. (Does anyone ever start a diet on Friday?) Holidays were my worst times. I started holiday-binging as early as Halloween when my children brought home their goodies. Their apparent lack of interest in the cache supplied me through Thanksgiving. So, I thought it best to start my diet after Thanskgiving. On second thought, that was a ridiculous idea, because it wasn't long until Christmas. After Christmas was the perfect time to start. But after Christmas, I realized that the New Year holiday was only a week away. Now, I made a New Year's resolution to lose weight, cleverly forgetting that my husband's birthday was January 4th. We always had ice cream and chocolate cake on that day! So, on January 4th, as I ate the birthday cake, I told myself that three more days didn't matter. But, after his birthday, I always bought a fresh supply of goodies. I had convinced myself that I was waiting for the right time to diet. For me, there was never a right time. Who was I kidding?

Today I have finally achieved normal weight, and I have maintained it. This was one of the most difficult and rewarding goals of all. I used all the principles in this book to accomplish it. Dieting alone is a Band-Aid method to treat a deeper problem. The thoughts you feed your mind are as important as the food you feed your body.

I decided I wanted to become a writer when I was in the first grade. I also dreamed of a college education. But, when I grew up and got a job, I told myself I couldn't accomplish those things and work too, so I decided to wait until I was married and could stay home.

After the children came along, I had another excuse: "I'll wait until they are grown and on their own." But in 1967, only a few months after the children left, I learned my husband had

Alzheimer's disease. Few knew very much about this disease, and I refused to believe it was fatal. Again I put my dreams on hold, devoting myself to his care, and telling myself I'd get on with things when he recovered. My husband lived for seven more years, and life was a nightmare. When I lost him, I felt I could not bear to go on living.

I had no dreams during this time. I was filled with fears. I developed many physical ailments. I became addicted to prescription drugs and alcohol. I no longer cared whether I got out of bed, and there were many days I didn't. I felt my spirit and my dreams were dead. But, I was wrong. I began to recover, first spiritually, then physically and mentally. My dreams reawakened. I knew I wanted a new career; one that would make a difference in the world, but I didn't know what it would be. I told myself I would get started very soon.

Six years later, when I was sixty-four, I attended a goal-setting seminar. I learned that I could write goals in every area of my life: physical, mental, emotional, spiritual, social, family, career and financial. I thought this was a great idea, but I didn't do anything about it until my sixty-fifth birthday. I decided on the career I wanted, and I wrote it down: **"I want to be a professional**

speaker and writer." No more excuses. I was on my own and had twenty-four hours a day to apply toward my goals. There was nothing and no one to stop me. Still I waited!

Why did I wait all those years for circumstances to be in my favor before I achieved my goals? **PROCRASTINATION!**

Suddenly, I realized the horrible truth. Procrastination had rooted itself in my nature from the time I was a child. It had been my constant companion and enemy all those years. I had lived an illusion all my life. I didn't have to wait until I was grown before developing myself; I didn't have to wait until I married, for the children to grow up, or for my husband to recover before pursuing my dreams. I was the only one in my way.

SECTION II

PROCRASTINATION WEARS MANY MASKS

CHAPTER 3

AVOIDANCE

Procrastination wears many masks. It is devious, cunning and sly. This ruthless, and deceptive enemy is a con-artist. It seduces you into believing it is your friend and benefactor while it robs you of your greatest treasure—**your life!** One reason we are deceived so easily is that all the masks are appealing, alluring and attractive. In the chapters that follow, we will remove the masks to expose the truth.

LET'S HAVE FUN!

Most, if not all of us, will agree that having fun is attractive. We are supposed to have fun. The more fun the better.

In her book, *Wake Up and Live*, Dorothea Brande relates a fable about a man who was promised health, wealth and happiness for the rest of his life if he would take a trip 100 miles north of his home. As he backed out of his driveway, he decided to take a short trip south first, just for fun. While on this detour, he ran out of gas, ran out of time, and missed his appointment in the north.

Do you like to go to a lot of parties? Take in all the new movies? Go to lunch with your friends? Talk on the telephone at length to everyone who calls, even if it's a wrong number? Read numerous magazines and newspapers? Read all the junk mail? Go shopping? Wouldn't you rather go directly to your appointment and realize your dreams while you still have gas and time?

YOU MUST KEEP BUSY

Our culture admires activity. It is believed the more active we are, the more successful we are. Consequently, we get caught in an activity trap that gives us a false sense of accomplishment. We rack up long hours and work diligently on low-priority jobs, move in many directions, and do not really accomplish anything of major importance. We complain about burnout and difficulty managing stress. But, much of our stress is self-produced. *Procrastination causes stress and anxiety*, while the high-priority jobs are still in the back of our minds, pestering us.

In a special report in *Success* magazine, Peter Turla and Kathleen Hawkins said there are two types of people: ant-stompers and elephant-hunters. Many of us are busy stomping ants. We go for the easy tasks that yield few benefits instead of the difficult ones that help us break through to our success.

I know a woman who spiels off all she has just done, with immense pride and a tone of martyrdom. The listener is likely to heave a sigh, saying: "How do you get all that done? I'm exhausted just hearing you tell it." She has a misguided feeling of accomplishment, when, beneath all this hurry and scurry, she has left the important things undone.

It isn't how busy you are that counts, but how much you accomplish.

MAKE A LIST

Successful people know it is important to list their goals. Research indicates that only three percent of the population write down their goals, and these people are the most successful. Keep in mind that *their success is due to the action they take to carry out their goals.* Be aware that list-making can be another of procrastination's many masks. It can become so attractive for some, they experience a false sense of achievement and list-making becomes their goal.

Refer to Chapter 7, for details about the five important lists for setting your goals.

READING

You might argue that you should be a prolific reader. That is true if you want to gain a general knowledge about many things, or if you read solely to be entertained. Reading, however, will not take you to your goal unless it is specialized reading in your field.

Robert Louis Stevenson said, "Books are good enough in their own way, but they are a mighty bloodless substitute for life." Needless to say, I was reading a book when I read that statement. Suddenly, my mind flashed back to my childhood when I first dreamed of writing a book. I had procrastinated for sixty-seven years. At this realization, I stopped reading and started writing. **The time comes to quit reading history and to make history.**

TELEVISION

Watching television may be the most attractive of all the masks.

A Phoenix, Arizona television station reported that over fifty people called the day after the October 1989 San Francisco earthquake to complain because they missed a situation comedy they referred to as "their" program. It was preempted by the earthquake news coverage. The television switchboard operator said she wouldn't repeat some of the words they used to express their anger.

Some people substitute watching television for achieving their goals. They spend hours, years, a lifetime watching others in action.

Television viewing can become an addiction. Stanton Peele, in *Love and Addiction*, reports the findings of the Society for Rational Psychology in Munich, Germany. When habitual viewers were denied their television, they experienced withdrawal symptoms, became disoriented, irritable with their families, and lost interest in sex.

I can't watch just a little television. In the past, I have told myself I would watch one or two good-quality programs and quit. But, I continued to switch from station to station to see what was next, and I ate constantly. So I not only wasted hours watching television, but I got fat. My solution was to store my television out of sight.

If watching television consumes hours of your time, it is important to look at where you are going with it. Has it become an addiction? This test will help you decide.

YOUR VIEWING HABITS

1. Do you turn people off when you turn television on?

2. Is it causing marital problems? Do you quarrel because of it?

3. Do you choose to watch television rather than spend prime time with your children or your mate?

4. Do you put off an important matter because you have to watch "your" program?

5. Do you ever watch television longer than you planned?

6. Do you watch television to escape worries and problems?

7. Are the people on the screen the kind of people you would invite into your home?

8. Do you need television to go to sleep?

9. Do you need it when you wake up and start your day?

10. Have you missed work to watch a special program?

11. Does watching television cause you to feel a loss of energy and ambition?

12. If you thought you could never watch television again would you be upset?

13. Have you called in sick because you are too tired to go to work after watching television all night?

14. Have you ever felt remorse over your viewing habits?

If you answered yes to more than three questions, television is usurping your personal power, which is one of the results of addiction.

I don't want to give the impression that I believe you shouldn't have fun or that the publishing and television industries should be abolished. These are not the culprits. They are symptoms. The problem occurs when you no longer control your life but allow these attractive activities to lure you away from reaching your goals.

SLEEPING

Does it surprise you that sleep can be an avoidance mechanism? People who are bored often sleep to avoid doing what needs to be done.

It is not my intention to advise you about how much sleep you need. Only you can decide this. If you worry about your sleeping habits, get medical attention. If there is no medical disorder that contributes to irregular sleeping habits, you may wish to consider the points made here.

If you have a dominant purpose for living, you are less likely to need much sleep. Many successful people sleep short hours because they get excited about what they are doing. They consider sleep a bother. Harry Truman, Lyndon Johnson, John F. Kennedy, Darwin, and Napoleon slept short hours. Thomas Edison averaged only four or five hours sleep in twenty-four.

When people have difficulty sleeping, their customary complaint is, "I'm so tired; I didn't sleep a wink all night." Yet, sleep studies suggest that these people sleep more than they think.

If you sleep short hours you may worry that you have insomnia. Instead of considering yourself deprived, you could look at this as additional hours for living. While the rest of the world sleeps, you can use this time for your most creative endeavors. These quiet hours are an opportunity for you to receive intuitive ideas. But they cannot take root in a field of worry and anxiety over lack of sleep.

FANTASIZING

James Allen wrote, "Dreamers are saviors of the world." It is true, that before you can plan a course of action, you must have a dream. However, some people think they are dreaming when they are really fantasizing. Fantasies are another attractive and captivating form of procrastination.

A good example is the many men and women who hate their work. A recent national poll revealed that ninety-five percent of all Americans do not enjoy their work. They are bored and feel so irritated that many escape into fantasies of self-employment. These people believe if they owned their own businesses, and became rich and famous, they would be happy. Yet, they continue to do the same job and make the same complaints, all the while talking about how things will be different someday. Life is so desolate and empty, they desperately need these fantasies because they have no hope of ever realizing anything different.

Lets take the opposite example. Others also feel frustrated and bored with work, dream of owning a business, and becoming rich and famous. But, these people are dreamers. They formulate in their minds what they wish to achieve. They work out plans for these dreams and write them down. These plans become their blueprints. They are committed to them. They enroll in management classes; read books on how to set up the business; and network with others to find out everything they can about owning a business. They make these choices instead of sitting in front of the television, going to the pub, or sitting around doing nothing and talking about nothing. They talk less about their dreams and do more to accomplish them.

Fantasizers are indolent, lack ambition, and have no hope of realizing their fantasies, while dreamers have mental pictures of expected results. Their commitment and faith in their dreams spur them into action.

WAITING FOR THE PERFECT TIME

I guess we think we are clairvoyant. Surely there is a better time to telephone a client or call on a customer. It's too early; he won't be up yet; he's out to lunch; he'll be in a meeting, ad infinitum.

We avoid doing things until vacation, Christmas, retirement, until the weather changes, until there is a full moon or a new moon. Maybe the right time is at the next eclipse. We wait until the economy picks up or interest rates go down. Winter is the best time--or is it summer?

If you have put your life on hold waiting for a perfect time, you are not alone. Believe me it's better to take action now instead of letting circumstances push you as they did me.

It had become my custom to celebrate my birthday by writing down my goals and making a "To Do" list. One year, in addition to new goals, I wrote down old goals that I had been listing for three years: put my house on the market and sell it; clean out my closet and throw out or give away clothes I no longer wore; and clean out the garage and basement. As I wrote these old goals down one more time, I felt sick, because I recognized one of procrastination's masks. I had fallen into the trap of list-making. After listing the old goals, I added new ones, and for the first time, I wrote at the top of the list: *"Overcome Procrastination."*

Early in the morning, two months later, I was reviewing my goals and "To Do" lists when my house caught fire. I called the fire department, and the voice at the other end asked, "Are you alone?" "Yes," I said. He commanded, "Hang up the phone and get out of the house, now!" He repeated firmly, "Hang up the phone and get out of the house **NOW!**" Do you think I procrastinated? Under other circumstances, you couldn't have gotten me to budge—I was still wearing a housecoat and hadn't put on my makeup. **BUT, YOU KNOW, I MOVED!**

After the firemen left, I stood in those charred ruins and thought, this fire was not on my "To Do" list. But it sure cleaned out my closet!

It was a big job to work in the wet ashes and the smell of smoke, and sort, inventory, pack and label my soggy, burned possessions. The things in the garage and basement hadn't burned. I found rusty tools I had purchased several years earlier for a fix-up job that I never got around to. I found my moth-eaten fishing bag with a fishing license pinned to it dated nine years earlier, ready for the fishing trip I was going to take *soon*. It fell apart in my hands like so much dust.

It took a life-and-death situation to get me to move immediately. I learned it is dangerous to wait for the perfect time. If you are waiting to go into action, I hope you don't wait so long that Life sets a fire under you to get you to move.

CHAPTER 4

I COULD HAVE...
I SHOULD HAVE...
IT'S TOO LATE

GUILT

When we were children my younger brother took great delight in teasing me. More than once, as I left the room and was just out of sight, he cried out, "Come back, I want to tell you something." I returned, to find him grinning impishly. "How far would you be if you hadn't come back?" he asked. Then he ran, squealing with glee, as I chased after him, swinging both fists; he always avoided my punch. I felt irritated and frustrated that he had conned me again. Today, these experiences are valuable lessons for me. When my mind does occasionally wander back to the past, I ask myself how far I would be if I hadn't gone back, and I promptly return to the present.

Some people ramble around in the past and torture themselves with guilt for things they could have done or for things they shouldn't have done.

Guilt is a useless emotion that squanders your life. Foisted upon us in infancy, guilt is used to discipline, control, and keep us moral. Instead, it demoralizes, lowers self-esteem and causes depression, and isolation.

You are emotionally and spiritually homeless when you feel you are unacceptable to yourself, your Creator, and others. Guilt keeps you shackled to the past and keeps you from doing anything worthwhile in the present.

There is a difference between excessive guilt and the natural reaction of regret. Be grateful that you have a conscience. Some people don't care if they have hurt others, and they never admit their wrong deeds. If you truly regret, make peace with the past and move on to the future. However, just wishing to feel free of guilt isn't enough. Here are some steps you can take.

1. Write about your guilt, then destroy the paper. What did you do? When? Who was affected besides you? What could you have done differently? What can you do now to make amends and restitution?

2. Ask forgiveness and close the process by forgiving yourself.

3. Set meaningful goals and start working on them today.

RELIVING PAST ACCOMPLISHMENTS

Has it occurred to you that reminiscing about the good times is a form of procrastination too?

It's pleasant to live in the after-glow of your accomplishments. But, this preoccupation stops you from defining new and higher goals. The idea is to learn from past performance for future use, not to invest emotion and energy in it by agonizing over it or lingering in elation.

A high achiever will not wait to hear whether the masses approved and does not run around town trying to find good reports of his work. He accomplishes more when he puts his mind to a new goal as soon as he has completed the previous one.

CRITICIZING OTHERS

Critics are not doers. Instead of taking action, they sit on the sidelines and direct. They are good at telling others how things should be done, but, when it comes to doing it themselves, they procrastinate.

These people need to see criticism for what it is: a cop out. If they expect others to change, they will never look at themselves. Every moment you spend criticizing others, you avoid developing yourself.

POURING YOUR LIFE INTO THE LIVES OF OTHERS

As I watched my husband's Alzheimer's condition progress, I began to realize that I would be alone very soon. I had never lived alone. One day I complained to my daughter, "I can't bear to think of living alone." She looked at me and said, "This will give you a chance to know who you really are." I had expected pity from her. Later I saw that her promise of self-discovery was more valuable than pity.

There are people who fear being alone as I did. Andre Gide' wrote, "Some of us are so afraid of finding ourselves alone that we never find ourselves at all." The last place they think to look for companionship is within themselves. Without a constructive purpose, they invest their lives in the lives of others and remain immature and unable to be on their own.

An example is the adult child who sacrifices his dreams to care for an apparently helpless, yet dominating, parent. On the other hand, some parents continue to care for the emotional, financial, and physical needs of their adult children. Whether the rescue is of the parent or of the adult child, the "virtuous" sacrifice is the same—martyrdom.

Our culture seems to admire martyrs. They are praised and considered saintly, so this is a captivating way to procrastinate. Whether serving or dominating, those who play the martyr have put their lives on hold.

It is important to be a caring child and a good parent. But, let this come from love, not from an unhealthy martyred stance. It's not possible to live your life and achieve your dreams while you put the interests and desires of others before your own.

JUST THIS ONCE WON'T HURT

We delay changing a habit when we rationalize, "Just this once won't hurt." "I'll start (or stop) tomorrow." What an illusion! Ask an alcoholic, an overeater, or a smoker who says, "Just this once won't hurt," yet keeps promising himself he'll stop drinking, overeating or smoking. After just one drink, the alcoholic has only one thing on his mind—the next drink. His tricky mind has forgotten the promise to have "Just one." For him it is not the second drink or tenth drink that does the damage, but the first.

So it is with a procrastinator. "Just this once" sets the procrastination habit deeper in your nature and you wait one more time to start.

The next time you tell yourself "Just this once," or if a well-meaning friend tries to convince you "Just this once won't hurt," ask yourself if this is procrastination wearing another attractive mask.

CHAPTER 5

ON TIME IS LATE

Tardiness is not usually recognized as procrastination. As a rule, people don't take it seriously. Yet, it adversely effects the life of the latecomer and the lives he touches.

Tardiness is an inconvenient, irritating and critical problem in business; yet, some managers tolerate it as though there were no alternatives.

Several years ago, a survey of 500 of the nation's largest companies was reported in *The Arizona Republic*. When asked what disturbed management the most about employee performance, tardiness appeared among the top complaints. One executive reported it didn't matter whether they opened their business at 9:00 or 10:00 a.m., some employees were always fifteen minutes late.

Some psychologists believe a chronic latecomer is hostile and rebellious to authority. He is unable to express anger in healthier ways and uses this technique to get even.

I was over sixty when I became aware that I used tardiness to rebel against authority. As early as I can recall, my mother fussed at me about being late. "You are as slow as cold tar," she scolded. Every time I dressed to go anywhere she hovered over me and warned that I would be late. When I went to school, she followed me out of the house and waved me on until I got out of sight. Those were painful experiences, and I unconsciously built up hostility. I stubbornly moved slower than ever! My mother's intentions were good. She did it out of love and a genuine concern that I develop good habits. She didn't know she would get reverse results, and neither did I. Unfortunately, I carried this behavior into my adult life. Much to my regret, I used the same tactics on my daughter.

If you use this technique on your children or anyone else you love, or on your employees, and you expect to get satisfactory results, I hope my personal experience will help you change your strategy.

THE PENALTIES FOR TARDINESS

Never having experienced the benefits of punctuality, a chronic late-comer would not believe the penalties for this behavior.

1. Tardiness is a Failure Technique — Some psychologists claim the late-comer sabotages himself because he fears success.

2. Tardiness Lowers Self-Confidence — Some late-comers "upstage" others to camouflage their low self-confidence. They display more charm than the occasion calls for with their quick-witted manner and unsolicited advice.

3. The Latecomer Misses Out — He can't find a parking place; he stands at the end of the line; he sits on the back row; the event is sold out; he misses planes, trains, buses, and boats. In spite of these penalties, the latecomer gets attention, and some prefer adverse attention to none at all. Others get a thrill out of breaking the rules. One young man told me he gets a kick out of being late. He likes to see if he can get away with it.

People who are persistently tardy often make an appeal for forgiveness and acceptance, yet they continue to arrive late as though, having made the appeal, they now have license to continue helpless and childlike behavior. They are unaware that they are responsible for their tardiness. They blame the traffic lights, the other drivers, or the weather—everything but themselves. Their insides are churning over these hindrances. This attitude works against them. Their frustration slows them down; they fumble and flounder, lose their keys, get speeding tickets, or worse, get in accidents.

The adage, "The hurrier I go, the behinder I get," is touchingly true for the person desperately trying to be on time.

FIVE WAYS TO OVERCOME TARDINESS

1. Imagine Yourself Arriving on Time

Comedian Flip Wilson said, "What you see is what you get." If a person doesn't believe this, he will unwittingly use his imagination to his detriment. For instance, he visualizes himself going in late and rehearses his entrance while rushing to his destination. What excuse will he give for being late? It must be good, so he elaborates on the truth or tells an out-and-out lie. Now he arrives in weakness instead of strength. He is out of control no matter how he tries to cover up. When he lies he undermines his integrity.

Use your imagination to your advantage. Practice seeing yourself arriving on time and in control.

2. Stop Making Excuses for Being Late

I'm not suggesting you be insensitive about the inconvenience you cause others. If an apology is in order, make it without giving an excuse and be done with it.

When you make excuses you reinforce the habit, confirm your reputation for being late, and lower your self-confidence. You continue to see yourself out of control. You become very good at making excuses. You are not only in the business of being chronically tardy, but now, you are in the excuse-making business.

Refuse to feel guilty, ashamed or discouraged. This compounds and reinforces the problem.

Instead, be optimistic and know you can and will unlearn the tardiness habit.

3. Make Positive Affirmations

Have you been saying:

"I'm afraid I'm going to be late."

"I'll never make it on time."

"I'm always late."

Catch yourself every time you make these statements and reverse them. In spite of evidence to the contrary, and especially if you are running late, say aloud:

"I'm in the right place at the right time."

"I'm known as being on time."

"I'm always on time."

"On time is late. I am always ten minutes early."

Press these positive affirmations into your subconscious mind every time you get ready to go somewhere and your subconscious will lead you to this type of behavior.

4. Say "No"

You are getting ready to leave your house. Someone knocks at your door uninvited; there is a telephone call of little importance; or a member of your household decides there is something that demands your attention. You *do* have the right to say "No" and continue on your way without feeling guilty or making excuses. When you learn to set your boundaries, eventually others will respect them.

5. Trim the Dead Wood Out of Your Life.

The following suggestion is vital to overcoming tardiness. If you feel this is of little importance, you are being deceived, and deception is one of procrastination's primary characteristics.

Pay attention to the many things you try to do before you leave. You may find that you are engrossed in useless motion. You know you should leave, but you are held as if magnetized. What would happen if you didn't do them? It will take some discipline to decide what's essential. If these things are essential do they have to be done just when you had planned to be somewhere where else?

CHAPTER 6

TAKE A CHANCE

Fear of taking risks is a serious form of procrastination. If you ever hope to achieve personal growth, you must take risks. We are born with curious natures. However, much of our wonder and natural desire to explore was lost when well-meaning parents tried to protect us. We were warned:

"Don't take any chances."
"Curiosity killed the cat."
"Fools rush in where angels fear to tread."
"Don't go where you are not wanted."

When we grow up, we take over and continue to say to ourselves:

"I can't be too careful these days."
"I know my limits."
"I'm not sticking my neck out."
"I'm playing it safe."

A woman who attended one of my seminars asked me how she could get started as a public speaker. "I don't want to take a wrong turn and go into the jungle and get scratched and bruised," she said. I responded, "Anyone who expects to explore the unknown without 'going into the jungle' and getting scratched and bruised will never take the journey."

History books are filled with cases of those who risked "going into the jungle" and brought great innovations to civilization. They not only got "scratched and bruised," but some were considered crazy and were persecuted, even put to death. Without the contributions of these people, where would technology be today? Medicine?

Education? The arts? Where would civilization be today?

Some people contend that it doesn't make sense to take risks. "That's not practical," they will argue. They use logic and reason to undertake a project. Risk-taking *is not* practical. Risk requires faith, and faith is not practical. William James wrote, "It is only by risking our persons from one hour to another that we live at all. Often our faith before hand in an uncertified result is the only thing that makes the result come true."

Use logic to make your plans as sound as possible. Make every effort to become knowledgeable about your project. Then develop the courage to step into the unknown with a quiet faith instead of fear. You can correct your course as you go. Be willing to accept the consequences.

OBSTACLES TO RISK-TAKING

The Need to Be Perfect

Some people will not take a chance because they fear they will make a mistake. They feel ashamed and embarrassed when they fail. They subscribe to the adage, "Anything worth doing is worth doing well." Who determines what "doing well" is? When we're concerned about our ability to do something well, we have a good excuse to do nothing at all. We are apt to think, "I might make a mistake, so I'd better forget it." I believe that anything worth doing is worth doing— **period**.

If you feel rooted in perfectionism, try the following steps to break through your deadlock.

1. Gather the best information you can and think it through. (Decide before hand when you will stop gathering information. Too much data can block you.)

2. Act on your decision. If the result is not everything you wanted it to be, don't call it a failure; call it a learning experience. Once started, you can usually make mid-course corrections. If you do fall flat on your face, have the resiliency to bounce back. Some people fall down and stay there so long they become attached to the place.

3. Move on to the next project. Do not give in to the tendency to rehash, rework, and regret the decision after launching the project.

The Need to Conform

There are those who do not want to appear different from the crowd. Because they want to fit in, they live a life of pretense. They think other people's thoughts, speak other people's words, and adopt other people's habits. If you disguise yourself because you fear criticism and rejection, you will lose touch with who you are. One man said, "I worked hard all my life to be somebody and, now that I have made it, it isn't me."

When you live a life of pretense, you are unable to make decisions, build faith in yourself, or develop courage. You will need all of these qualities when you take risks.

The Fear of Insecurity

A man who was putting off a new venture, said he was afraid to give up the security of his present job. "I wouldn't mind taking a chance if I were sure it would work," he said. There is no risk in a sure thing. If you insist on security, you will make a prisoner of yourself. If you remain in your safety zone, you won't be free to move into the unknown or to explore new arenas.

You can develop the courage to take risks by making positive affirmations:

"I have fun exploring."
"I enjoy taking risks."
"I am more creative when I take chances."

I like Charles Lamb's statement, "It's good to love the unknown."

Fear of Fear

A certain amount of fear is necessary for survival. When used correctly it gives the warnings necessary for self-preservation. A sky diver said he is skeptical of anyone who claims to be so courageous that he lacks fear. "He would be dangerous to work with."

For years I heard the saying: "If you do the thing you fear doing, the fear will leave you," but I didn't understand this until I became a public speaker. I was terrified to speak at first. I stumbled and stuttered and felt embarrassed. But, I persisted. Today, when I speak before an audience, I become so exhilarated, I don't want to stop.

Fear is a paradox: If you allow it to immobilize you, you will remain insecure and uncertain. But if you force yourself to act, the fear will be transformed into anticipation and excitement.

HOW TO GET STARTED

If you want to raise your level of risk-tolerance, start small and you will build confidence for larger, more important risks.

Will you risk dressing according to your taste, or do you wear fashions unbecoming to you? Worse yet, are they uncomfortable? I admire Katherine Hepburn who preferred wearing slacks instead of dresses. In his book, *Tracy & Hepburn,* Garson Kanin tells of a London hotel that had a "no-ladies-in-trousers" rule and requested that Katherine wear a dress; she replied she didn't have one and continued to wear slacks.

I know a man who loves to dance. Yet, he won't risk being the first one on the dance floor. If no one dances, he misses the entire number.

Will you take the risk to laugh when no one else laughs, or do you become embarrassed and try to smother it? I witnessed this when I presented a three-hour seminar with some really funny stories that past audiences had enjoyed. I commented to a friend who had been in this audience that this group had not laughed as much as the others. She confided that she wanted to laugh but had contained the urge because no one else did, and she felt awkward.

These are examples of small risks you can take, and, despite the outcome, you will receive certain rewards. You will change your personality. You will raise your self-esteem, build faith, and improve your ability to make decisions.

SECTION III

KICK THE HABIT

CHAPTER 7

BREAK OUT OF
YOUR SHELL!

Now that you recognize the devious and subtle ways this ruthless, yet attractive, enemy cunningly contrives to deceive you, let's look at the techniques you can use to kick procrastination out of your life.

FIND YOUR PURPOSE

The easiest way to kick the procrastination habit is to find your purpose in life. Once you find your purpose, nothing will stop you from reaching your goals. You will be filled with a burning desire that will take you to your destination.

Almost every person eventually comes to the age-old question: Why am I here? What is my purpose? When they don't know the answer, they become restless and discontented.

Most people believe the solution to this dilemma is to find the right partner, the right job, the right home, or to make more money. They try to find satisfaction in possessions, power, and in the approval of others.

They spend a lifetime trying to get more of the very things that aren't working for them, and more is never enough. They don't realize they are procrastinating when they substitute getting for becoming. They remain unhappy, confused, and dissatisfied. This dissatisfaction is the longing for a sense of fulfillment and purpose.

If you are to find your purpose, you must make your own decisions. Allowing others to make your decisions will cause confusion and indecisiveness. Believe in your ability to receive intuition and inspiration. Listen to your inner voice. Once you know your purpose and establish your code of moral values, it does not matter whether or not others agree. You are now on your own path, not one that someone else laid out for you.

A young man once told me he couldn't decide what single thing he most wanted to do. "One day I think I want to be a free-lance writer," he said. "The next, I think I want to be an electrical engineer. On the other hand, I would like to be an actor." He starts one project, gets it partly finished, loses interest, and starts another. This is similar to a farmer who plows and sows one field after another and never remains to reap the harvest.

If you feel stranded in indecision, ask yourself the following questions and write down your answers. What is really most important to me? Where am I going? How will I get there? How much time and effort am I willing to spend reaching my goals?

If these questions were difficult, here are four techniques you can use to help you decide what you want to do.

1. Make Positive Affirmations

Stop making negative affirmations about your indecision, such as:

"I can't make up my mind."

"I don't know what to do."

"Just as sure as I make a decision, it's bound to be wrong."

Establish a field of expectancy by replacing these negative affirmations with positive ones:

"I am getting better and better at making wise and sound decisions."

"I have made a firm, irreversible decision."

Your response to these suggestions may be, "You've got to be kidding me; that's not true." This is a normal reaction. You have been pro-gramming your subconscious mind with negative affirmations, and your conscious mind (which is logical and reasoning) tells you these positive statements are not true. On the other hand, your subconscious mind takes whatever statements you make and manufactures them according to your specifications. Like a robot, it does not reason.

Therefore, it doesn't know the difference between the real and the imagined. So, keep sending it positive statements and use your imagination to see them coming true. Be persistent and patient and, in time, they will be true.

2. Pay Attention To Your Good Ideas

You may say, "I never get a good idea." You might even argue for your limitations and say you are stupid. If you don't consider your idea valuable purely because it's yours, you will get sidetracked or toss it out.

On the other hand, if you do recognize that your idea is worthwhile and put it aside until you get around to it, you are procrastinating. Why? Because each delay develops the losing habit of procrastination. When you immediately act on an idea, new energy is released and that idea generates more ideas. If, after making the decision, things are not going well, do not assume you made a wrong decision. Not all decisions are immediately rewarding. It is important to develop a tolerance for ambiguity. It may take time for you to produce results. The only wrong decision is no decision at all.

3. Develop Concentration

We behave like young children when we start several things and never finish any of them. Like a bee, darting from flower to flower, we delightfully dart from one interest to another, seeing, smelling, hearing, tasting, and enjoying the exciting distractions. When we let these distractions lure us from finishing what we start, we are incapable of concentrating on one thing for very long.

It was said that Helen Keller, although deaf, blind and mute, always finished what she started. Because she was deprived of the sights and sounds that delight and distract others, she was able to concentrate. She said, "Thank God for my handicaps; without them, I would not have succeeded." Dr. Vernon Mark, in his book *Brain Power*, said that, like any other learned behavior, we can develop the ability to avoid distractions and increase our skill of concentration.

If you want to improve your power of concentration, spend quiet time alone each day. Discipline your mind to focus on one thing at a time. This exercise in concentration may be difficult at first; but, if you develop the daily habit, it will eventually lead you to the answers you seek. Trust the brilliant ideas that emerge. They come from your intuitive mind. Eventually, your intuitive mind will disclose to you the one thing you want to do more than any other. Then go into action on it immediately.

4. Write

The simple act of writing down your ideas proves you are a decision-maker. You made a decision to write. As you continue this practice, confidence in your ability to make decisions improves.

It is very important to capture your ideas on paper. Keep a notebook handy so you can jot down your ideas before they evade you. If you discipline yourself to write your ideas and goals, it will be easier to discipline yourself to take action.

FIRST THINGS FIRST

Once you know what you want to do, give priority to your personal values and ethical system. Guard against going along with the crowd and letting the values of others take precedence. Do not compromise yourself.

When you develop a passion for your life's work, you will become so committed it will be easy to determine the things that are most important and to bypass those of little significance.

SET YOUR GOALS

You must set goals if you are to fulfill your purpose.

1. List goals for all areas of your life: physical, mental, emotional, spiritual, family, social, career, and financial.

   Balance is important. Check each area to see if you invest more of your time and energy in one and neglect the others. Some people set goals to build up their bodies and neglect their spiritual development. Others are more interested in wealth, and devote all their time to their careers.

   When you took the Procrastination Self-Test in Chapter 1, did you feel question 8 belonged? Are you aware that a workaholic can be a procrastinator? It is common for people to place most of their emphasis on professional goals. If they do this to the exclusion of their mental, physical, and spiritual development, they can become addicted to the work process and their lives get out of balance. They tell themselves they will get around to their personal lives later when they are not so busy with work or when they retire. When they do retire, they don't know how to find meaning in their lives. They don't know how to relax or play; their families have made a life without them; they have physical ailments; and the work that gave meaning to their lives is now gone.

A few years ago I read that the president of a financial institution was unhappy about his "forced retirement." In an interview, he said, "One day you're somebody, and the next day, you're nobody."

If you make wealth, fame and power your only aim, while putting other things on the back burner, procrastination has conned you again.

2. List the obstacles to your goals. When you get them on paper, you may realize they are myths. Now, list possible solutions to these obstacles. You may find they are not as difficult as you thought. With practice, you will come up with more than one unusual and creative solution. Decide which one is the most likely to work, then go into action on it.

3. List the benefits you will enjoy when you reach your goal. What are they? Travel? Personal growth? New and successful friends and associates? Better health? Improved relationships? Improved lifestyle? These are real motivators. If you do not see any benefits, you will not be motivated to achieve your goals.

Continue to work with this list. As you do, you will think of benefits that would not have occurred to you at first.

4. Make a time schedule. How much time will you spend on high priority projects? Don't lock yourself into this schedule. Use it to help you become aware of how you spend your time.

5. Make a "To Do" List. Give each item a priority (such as A, B, C). Be careful to stay with those tasks that have the highest priority. When you feel bogged down with a project on your A list, it is very tempting to skip to an easier task on your lower-priority B or C lists.

CUT GOALS INTO BITE-SIZE PIECES

If your goals are too big or your dreams too remote, they will not appear realistic. You will have difficulty getting your mind around them and you will put them off because they will seem impossible. To avoid this problem, divide the project into small sections: make the first phone call; set the first appointment; write the first letter, memo, or chapter; give the first speech.

Once you do this, you will feel new energy. This energy creates more energy, and the momentum will keep you going as you practice daily. When you succeed in one small goal, your confidence increases. With one success behind you, you are a different person and better equipped to take the second step. The way to establish new habits is one at a time, one day at a time.

MAKE A COMMITMENT, READY OR NOT

Most people will not make a commitment because they are unsure of the future. Some people will not even commit themselves to twenty-four hours in the future.

You may fear making a commitment because you feel you need more time and information to get your plans in place. But, if you make the commitment you will be forced to get the plans firmed up.

As a member of Toastmasters International, I invite visitors to join. Often, they say "I'd like to speak like you Toastmasters, but I'm not ready yet. I'd have to build up my confidence first." Well, they have it backward! Once they get up and speak, they will be more confident. The principle is the same in anything you do. Once you make a commitment, you will get ready.

BE WILLING TO SUFFER

"Who wants to suffer?" you ask. No one. Yet you cannot remain in your comfort zone, feel safe and secure, enjoy all the attractive procrastination techniques we have discussed, and expect your life to change.

It is painful to break established habits, so expect to feel pain and frustration when you begin to kick the procrastination habit.

USE WHAT YOU HAVE

When I first began to change my life, I attended seminars, and self-help groups, read self-help books, and listened to motivational cassette tapes. After I decided to become a speaker and writer, I joined several associations. I went to one seminar after another. I sat in the audience for hours, soaking up all the information I could to further my career. I absorbed information but didn't dispense it. These activities were necessary to a point, but the time came for me to get out of the audience and onto the platform. I went to fewer meetings, lectures and seminars, and put a moratorium on buying cassette tapes and books until I used what I had. I also cancelled eight of my twelve magazine subscriptions.

I finally began to carry out the suggestions made in the materials that were stacked up in my home gathering dust.

I would like you to try an exercise. Go back in your life and take an inventory of the information you have gathered, the training you have received, and the time, money, and energy you have invested in a goal that interested you and you have now abandoned. Your investment may not be wasted. Is something gathering dust that you could salvage and use to take you where you want to go?

Do not let this become an exercise in remorse. If you are no longer interested, it is appropriate to let it go and move on with no regrets. On the other hand, if you can use it, dust it off and put it to work in your life.

SAY "NO" WITHOUT GUILT OR EXCUSES

It is so common for people to allow others to choose their careers, mates, religion, friends, place of residence, size of family, what they eat and how they dress.

As children, we were taught to be polite. We learned how to say "Yes" when we wanted to say "No." We learned how to say "Thank you" when we didn't mean it. We were told what to do and when to do it.

Granted, we needed training and guidance from those responsible for us. But this pattern, subconsciously established in childhood, can become a life-long habit of dependency on others to make our decisions and solve our problems.

If you are still afflicted with this dependency habit, you will prefer the approval of others over your success. To find out how serious this problem is in your life, consider the following:

CHECK LIST FOR SAYING "NO"

1. Do you allow others to make plans for you without consulting you first?

2. Have you followed a career someone else decided you should have?

3. Have you married the person someone else decided was best for you, or not married because someone else decided it wasn't a good match?

4. Do you belong to a church that someone else chose for you? Would you be considered a heretic or a "black sheep" if you left it?

5. Is the size of your family determined by opinions and morals of others?

6. Do you let someone else decide what food you will eat because you can't hurt their feelings by refusing?

7. Does someone else decide what you will wear?

Some people live in terror of what may happen if they say "No." They might be considered selfish. They don't want to hurt anyone's feelings. They might lose a friend.

You betray yourself if you say "Yes" when you want to say "No." You have put the values of others before your own. You lose your autonomy and personal power, a high price to pay for the approval of others!

Keep in mind that saying "No" after years of saying "Yes" will demand determination and persistence on your part. You won't be taken seriously at first. Others may wheedle and beg and accuse you of not loving them. Do not yield to this type of domination. It becomes easier to say "No" if you have made a decision to be true to yourself and to your values.

Promises, Promises

Making unasked for promises lightly and foolishly is closely related to the inability to say "No."

This frequently happens in the work place. If a co-worker is having difficulty on the job, do you offer to set your work aside (procrastinate) to help. If you perceive the boss needs an extra hand, do you perform a rescue mission, miss your own work deadline, and end up behind the eight ball? Then, do you become resentful because nobody appreciates you?

I was a rescuer early in my career, and it cost me my job. A young woman, hired as my assistant, was concerned about being fired because she could not learn the work. I volunteered to help her secretly. I gave her my new typewriter and took her old one. My work suffered. The result was I had volunteered myself right out of a job. Her work looked so much better than mine, I was the one dismissed when it came time to cut personnel. I bitterly resented her and the company. More than forty-five years later, when I took personal responsibility for my choices, I realized I had done it to myself.

Some habits die hard. I vowed I would never again voluntarily make promises that would affect me adversely. But, I did it again recently. During a telephone conversation with a friend, I spontaneously volunteered to mail some information. He hadn't asked me for it; he didn't even know I had it. This may seem a perfectly innocent thing to do, but it cost time that was dear to me. I searched for several hours and couldn't locate the material. I finally had to call him and renege on my promise. I had wasted precious time I could have spent on the manuscript my editor was waiting for.

Take Charge

If you don't plan your time and your life, someone else will. Others are eager to make your plans and schedule your activities. When this occurs, you are apt to feel pressured. This is less likely to happen if you have written goals and scheduled completion dates.

If you wish to be an emotionally healthy and mature individual, resign from the people-pleasing business and refuse to compromise yourself. Take charge of your life and make your own choices.

"Time is the coin of life," wrote Carl Sandberg, "You spend it. Do not let others spend it for you."

SEIZE OPPORTUNITIES

A procrastinator walks right past opportunities. Why?

• Opportunities require action; they are swift and fleeting, and procrastinators are passive.

• Procrastinators complain about their problems and don't recognize their opportunities.

• Procrastinators concentrate on smaller, less important matters. Once committed, they can't change their plans to allow for greater opportunities.

- Sometimes it is difficult to recognize an opportunity. Much like a diamond in the rough, it may be hidden in an unexpected or unattractive form.

- Procrastinators feel intimidated by the challenges that opportunities offer.

When you see an opportunity, seize it before it's too late. You may never see it again!

STOP TALKING AND TAKE ACTION

Become a doer, not a talker. Do you know people who go on and on about all the things they have to do? They cite it all, never skipping a beat, and are out of breath when they finish.

Do you frequently voice your seemingly innumerable, ever-present tasks? If so, I assure you that you will not get them done. Why? Because this activity drains your energy and wastes your time. The next time you have the urge to do this, repress it. Notice your increased energy and productivity.

DEVELOP COMPASSION FOR YOURSELF

How many children are told they are dummies when they don't get A's in school? They grow up feeling worthless because their value is determined by their performance. As a result, few adults have genuine compassion for themselves. If you don't believe it, check out some of the things they say. "What a fool I am." "I could kill myself for doing that." "I never could do anything right." "I'm no good." "I'm a nobody."

When you reject yourself you are procrastinating. You cannot become the kind of person you want to become as long as you dislike who you are now. You won't see yourself accomplishing anything as long as you remind yourself and others of your incompetence and shortcomings. You are valuable as you are. Failure to succeed has nothing to do with your self-worth. Don't make the mistake of tying your performance to your view of yourself.

When you feel as if you have blundered and are filled with remorse or shame, say to yourself, "Okay, so I made a mistake; I can do better the next time, and I will." Don't wait until the next time to think it through. Use your imagination to visualize yourself doing it better right now. This will help you become more successful each time you find yourself in a similar situation. Eventually you will succeed because you have mentally practiced it ahead of time. This unconditional self-acceptance is the compassion you need to develop into the person you want to become. Beating up on yourself will keep you where you are.

Promise yourself that you will guard your tongue and your thoughts and never put yourself down again. This will take self-discipline, but it will pay off. The internal wars will stop; your self-image will improve and you will accomplish more.

CHAPTER 8

YOU ARE DESIGNED FOR SUCCESS

If you are applying the suggestions in this book and are not progressing as you think you should, don't feel discouraged. If you backslide don't be disappointed. Remember to use compassion. With practice you will succeed!

In *Psycho Cybernetics*, Dr. Maxwell Maltz said we are goal-oriented organisms designed to succeed. He claims God did not engineer his product to fail. He is saying you were born to win.

Be patient with yourself and persist. Persistence will determine whether you succeed or fail. None of the suggestions offered in this book will be of any use without persistence.

In addition to persistence, the following four principles are vital prerequisites to your success.

1. KEEP AN OPEN MIND

There are many ways to look at things, but some people close their minds and think there is only one right way—and that right way is their way. To them things are all black or all white, and they become emotional when their beliefs are threatened by opposite views. As children, they formed concepts based on the fantasies, emotions, stereotypes, and prejudices of those in authority. Some of the concepts were irrational and didn't work; yet, it was risky business to look at new and reverse ideas.

Some ideas and suggestions in this book may represent a threat to your old, well-established beliefs and habits.

If you wonder whether you are open-minded, did you become angry, indignant, or rebellious at any ideas presented in this book? When presented with new evidence, can you change a belief or habit or at least investigate without contempt? If so, you are an open-minded person. You possess one of the characteristics necessary to overcome procrastination.

2. BE WILLING

Overcoming procrastination is a do-it-yourself job, and it will be one of the most difficult, yet rewarding, jobs you ever do.

How badly do you want to whip procrastination? Are you willing to go to any length to apply the techniques in this book? Sometimes we think we want something with all our hearts, but if a great storm comes into our lives, or even a little rain; if we have setbacks or disappointments, we give up and revert to our old ways.

3. DEVELOP A DESIRE

There seems to be a general belief that people of achievement have exceptional talents and special genius. They are believed to be lucky and life seems easy for them. On the contrary. All great achievers reached the pinnacle of success after first overcoming defeat. When adversities and failures took them down, they rose again and again. When others gave up on their dreams, these people toiled over theirs. When it appeared their dreams wouldn't survive, they sat through the long night of darkness, nursing them. They kept their dreams alive. Their dreams became greater than the dreamers.

Do you have a desire to overcome procrastination? I don't mean a milquetoast, mediocre, maybe I will and maybe I won't attitude, but a burning desire? Do you have the kind of desire that generates enthusiasm, energy, and commitment; the kind of desire that will spur you on to take chances and risk change when others play it safe; the kind of desire that will keep you going in the face of tragedy and failure?

The following guidelines will help you develop a burning desire, and you will persevere when others have gotten off track.

Find a Purpose

"Find Your Purpose" is the first step set forward in Chapter 7, and it is first for a reason. Without a constructive purpose, you are a target for boredom and worries. Finding your purpose is the foundation upon which all other principles in this book are built. When you apply these principles, you will have the power to move beyond procrastination and to fulfill your purpose.

Dream

People who are analytical and logical do not give much credence to dreamers. They consider them idle and aimless. This is not true. Dreams are for ambitious, concerned and alive people. If you hold your dreams in high regard and protect them against the barbs and doubts of others, they will help you generate a white heat of desire.

Visualize

Use your imagination to project your dreams on the screen of your mind. Visualize them in detail for a preview of coming attractions.

Positive Self-Talk

Tell yourself you are for yourself. Be your own champion for success.

See the Benefits

Remind yourself of the benefits you will enjoy once you reach your goal.

4. HAVE A PLAN

Prepare a detailed plan in the form of written goals. Ask yourself what you would like to do and write it down on a card. Place it where you can see it the first thing in the morning and the last thing at night.

It takes practice to break out of the prison of a firmly established habit. Habit is the key that locked the prison door. Habit will unlock it. Eventually, new and better habits will root themselves in your nature just as procrastination did.

Be patient and compassionate with yourself and persist. One day you will wake up and realize you have moved beyond procrastination.

BIBLIOGRAPHY

A Personal Achievement Guide to Time Management, Peter A. Turla and Kathleen L. Hawkins, SUCCESS, November, 1981.

The Addictive Organization, Anne Wilson Schael and Diane Fassel, Harper & Rowe, San Francisco, California.

Age Wave, Ken Dychtwald, J.P. Tarcher, Los Angeles, California.

The Art of Selfishness, David Seabury, Pocket Books, New York, New York.

As a Man Thinketh, James Allen, DeVorss & Company, Marina del Rey, California.

Brain Power, Vernon Mark, M.D., Houghton Mifflin Company, Boston, Massachusetts.

Chancing It. Why We Take Risks, Ralph Keyes, Little Brown and Company, Toronto, Canada.

Compassion & Self-Hate, Theodore Isaac Rubin, Ballantine Books, New York, New York.

Do What You Love, The Money Will Follow: Discovering Your Right Livelihood, Marsha Sinetar, Paulist Press, New York, New York.

Eight Deadly Sins, ARIZONA REPUBLIC, *January 6, 1985 (AP NY).*

How to Get Control of Your Time and Your Life, Alan Lakein, Signet, New York, New York.

If you Meet the Buddha On the Road, Kill Him! Sheldon B. Kopp, Bantam Books, New York, New York.

Love and Addiction, Stanton Peele, New American Library, Inc., New York, New York.

Man's Search For Meaning, Viktor E. Frankl, Simon & Schuster, New York, New York.

Overcoming Procrastination, Albert Ellis and William J. Knaus, New American Library, Inc., New York, New York.

Positive Addiction, William Glasser, Harper & Rowe, New York, New York.

Power of the Subconscious Mind, Joseph Murphy, Prentice-Hall, Inc. Englewood Cliff, New Jersey.

Psycho-Cybernetics, Maxwell Maltz, Prentice-Hall, Englewood Cliff, New Jersey.

Tracy & Hepburn, Garson Kanin, Primus (B.I. Fine), New York, New York.

Wake Up and Live, Dorothea Brande (Although this book is out of print, you may find it worthwhile to do some detective work to find it.)

When I Say No, I Feel Guilty, Manuel J. Smith, Bantam Books, New York, New York.

INDEX

W

LET ME HEAR FROM YOU

I would love to hear about your successes or your problems in moving beyond procrastination. I also welcome your questions.

Write me at:

Moving On Publications
924 E. Westchester Drive
Tempe, AZ 85283

ABOUT THE AUTHOR

A full-time professional speaker and columnist, Virginia Granger is a member of Toastmasters International, the National Federation of Press Women, and the National Speakers Association. Virginia is the recipient of the "1985 MEMBER OF THE YEAR" award from the Arizona Chapter of the National Speakers Association.

Because she speaks from experience, Virginia Granger is an exciting and inspiring speaker and seminar leader. She provides training in a number of areas you can utilize in your personal life and in your business. She uses metaphors, allegories, legends and myths, spiced with humor for effective learning. She tailors the program to your special needs. If your organization is interested in sponsoring her lectures, workshops or seminars, please direct inquiries to:

VIRGINIA GRANGER SEMINARS
MOVING ON PUBLICATIONS
924 E. WESTCHESTER DRIVE
TEMPE, AZ 85283

ORDER FORM

Send____copies of HOW YOU CAN MOVE
BEYOND PROCRASTINATION @ $7.95 ea.

$_____

Arizona residents add 6 1/2% sales tax:_____

Shipping and handling: _____
(Add $2.00 shipping and handling for the
first book; $1.50 for each additional.)

Total Payment Enclosed
(Check or Money Order): $_____

How You Can Move Beyond Procrastination is
available in quantity discounts. Please write for
more information.

MONEY BACK GUARANTEE

Name:_____

Address:_____

City_____ State_____ Zip_____

SEND ORDER TO:
        Moving on Publications
        924 E. Westchester Drive
        Tempe, Arizona 85283-30__

finished 6/12/2000 JHR
finished 6/14/2000 JHR
finished 6/16/2000 JHR